CONT

INTRODUCTION

This book may not turn you into the
next Bill Gates, nor even make you a
million, but it might just give you some
idea of just how useless you can be and still
progress up the corporate ladder, provided you
know the lingo. Management is all about bullshit,
and the language known as management-speak:
once you have this mastered you'll be able to
hide behind all sorts of gross incompetence.
And this book will teach you all you need to
know, in just seven days, for just £4.99! Better
than paying several hundred quid to watch
some 'motivator' come over from America,
just to tell you the bleeding obvious anyway.

What is management-speak?

Management-speak, Jargonese and Corpspeak are all names given to a particular form of English used in business and government. Its main characteristics are waffle, the use of long, complicated words when a short one would do, and the use of mixed metaphors, often borrowed from the world of the military. Bullshit and euphemism are also central to this dialect, which is why it has passed seamlessly from the military to business and politics. A professor of Princeton University, Harry G. Frankfurt, even brought out a report called *On Bullshit*, which led one reviewer to comment darkly about a 'world bullshit take-over'.

HOW TO BE A BULLSHIT MANAGER IN 7 DAYS

Crombie Jardine
PUBLISHING LIMITED
Office 2, 3 Edgar Buildings
George Street
Bath
BA1 2FJ
www.crombiejardine.com

Copyright © Crombie Jardine Publishing Limited, 2006

First published by Crombie Jardine Publishing Limited, 2006

ISBN 1-905102-56-9 (10-digit)

ISBN 978-1-905102-56-3 (13-digit)

Written by Edward West
Edited by Christine Rista
Designed by www.glensaville.com
Printed and bound in Great Britain by
William Clowes Ltd, Beccles, Suffolk

The History of Bullshit

Languages develop when a group becomes so
separated from the rest of the population that
its members begin to communicate in a way
that is incomprehensible to outsiders. Cockney
rhyming slang, for example, developed so that
non-East Enders couldn't tell what criminal
activity the chirpy wheezing rascals were up to;
Polari was spoken by gay men in the days when
homosexuality was a crime, and such speakers
as Kenneth Williams and Larry Grayson cleverly
managed to pass themselves off as red-blooded
ladies' men. Management-speak has developed
as a way of ensuring that no one outside
the meeting room, and often few of those
inside, understand what the hell is going on.

Managerialism can be traced back to the 1930s, but the current jargon that drives us all insane is more recent. It originated in large corporations and business schools in the United States in the 1980s, during the 'total quality management' movement. Management-speak English (or MSE[1]) as it is now known, has become so endemic in Britain as to completely take over many industries, central and local government, as well as major public bodies such as the BBC and the NHS. The probable cause of this take-over was the outsourcing (itself an MSE word) of roles to a new class of management consultants, outside 'experts' who travelled from company to company, spreading their language in the same way as a council estate Lothario spreads Chlamydia around a Greek holiday resort.

---

[1] For the sake of convenience, I may call management-speak MSE from time to time. It saves space, and, as we all know, managers love turning any phrase into a set of initials.

Management-speak has become so popular, in fact, that several words and phrases have leaked into the English language, such as 'no brainer' and 'leverage.' Tesco supermarkets now even sell ready-meals with names like 'Chinese meal solutions', just in case any middle managers out there have become so cut off from reality that they can't understand food labels written in normal English, and risk experiencing a 'starving to death outcome' as a result.

Number of speakers

Anywhere between 10,000 and 10 million
at any one time, mainly in the United
States and Britain, and concentrated in
the M4 business corridor, White City,
Westminster and the home of former
BBC Director-General John Birt.

Usage

The language helpfully comes in pre-fabricated blocks of words that can be lumped together to form sentences, since the normal rules of grammar do not apply, and no one's going to understand anyway. Management-speakers also love to turn a noun into a verb. Pretty much any noun can be changed in this way, so don't be surprised to see unlikely contenders such as 'flagpole' or 'shit-face' verbified in the near future.

Pronunciation

Since management-speak originated in America, users often develop a strange mid-Atlantic accent when using it, and for this reason I have kept the American 'z' rather than the British 's' when spelling some of the gobbledegook words of this dictionary.

A final note: all the references to Latin and Middle English in the context of a word's origins are true, although Biblical quotes may have been slightly bullshitized in order to jocularize the situation.

If you can't beat 'em, join 'em

So forget all those English lessons you learnt at school – these days managers speak a different language altogether, and if you want to become one of them, you'll have to learn to speak bullshit. With this small guide, you should manage it in just seven days.

MONDAY

TOUCHING BASE

Proof that management-speak has evolved into a separate language comes from the fact that several British universities, Sheffield and Birmingham among them, teach impressionable youngsters how to use words like 'synergize', 'functionalities' and 'infomediaries' through degrees in management. It makes you wonder if any of the students have ever pondered, 'Ah, living in Birmingham and learning Leisure Management – can life get any better than this?' But remember – if it weren't for all the universities teaching management skills, Britain's economy would collapse overnight, and the nation would end up with a similar GDP to that of Haiti or Burkina Faso.

After obtaining their degree, the students' best bet is to join a firm of management consultants, often starting with a poverty-reducing six months unpaid internship, where they will be taught all the skills necessary for walking into someone else's office and telling them how to run things. So, the first lesson must be to learn the basic terms of bullshit, the tools no self-respecting wannabe David Brent can do without.

BULLSHIT MANAGER'S

MONDAY SPEAK

Alpha The most important, from the Greek letter 'A' – implying that something vaguely important is 'beta' or even 'epsilon', and that something of 'omega' importance can be left to the intern.

Analogous With 'to' added on, an important-sounding version of 'like', in the old sense of the word, before it came to mean 'said' by inarticulate young Americans.

B2B Back-to-back. Consecutive. A management-speak phrase that works as a text message (though it's difficult to think of a situation where teenagers might use it) perhaps along the lines of 'G8 B2B qtly sls fgrs Kevin x' – i.e. Great back-to-back quarterly sales figures.

Back-end The end of the (financial) year, March. When the first shoots of spring arrive, the taxman starts sniffing around for irregularities, and the director awards himself £250m in share options.

Best-of-breed A service so good that it could be compared to a scrubbed and manicured thoroughbred Dalmatian with exactly 101 spots.

Box Where innovative people do their thinking. Those who think outside the box might consider themselves freethinking company mavericks that want to live fast and die young, to hell with conventions. Of course, everyone else thinks they're tossers, but that's irrelevant.

Brand Once only brands had a brand, now a brand is applied to anything, including charities, government departments and religions. Even the nation itself is often called UK PLC by lisping senior politicians intent on 'selling the country'. Soon, even the likes of Fallujah and Chernobyl will no doubt have a marketing team trying to sell them as a 'brand', however hopeless the cause.

Change Drivers Forces, both human and non-human, that make things happen, and possibly alter future courses of marketing divisions in various alternative realities. When the history of the world is rewritten in management-speak, Ghandi, Che Guevara and Hitler will all be lumped together as 'innovative change drivers'.

Clicks and mortar A clever pun on 'bricks and mortar', which somehow implies that playing with a mouse is the sort of rugged profession that would get Lady Chatterley all worked up.

Convergence Referring to a point on a graph with the words 'Quarter One, 2021' beside it; where one line meets another, usually in a futuristic dark patch on the right hand with 'predicted' next to it.

Core business/core policy/core strategy The company activities that actually make money, not the bits it pretends to care about for the sake of public relations.

Due diligence More of a management cliché than actual MSE, but nonetheless a fancy, overused way of saying 'we'll do our best.'

Enable One of the dozen or so most common MSE words, encapsulating the go-getting, 'can do but need to go through all the procedures first' attitudes so beloved of management types.

Essence As in 'brand essence'. Another, more spiritual, way of saying the company's advertising slogan. Thus some four words phrase thought up by an advertising agency becomes something greater than a mere motto, it captures the heart and soul of the product.

Event A superfluous word that could be applied to absolutely anything, from an asteroid hitting the Earth, to going to the toilet.

Fast track A verb that conjures up someone cruising down the outer lane of life in a flash Italian sports car. In other words, a university graduate with a degree in transport management who has suddenly been put in charge of ten people twice his age. A berk with a degree.

Feedback 1. The horrible noise that emanates from an amplifier that has been switched on too loud. 2. Your carefully considered opinions on your boss's latest plan.

Front-end 1. Money paid up-front, in the belief that if the service is provided first payment may not be forthcoming, suggesting that your service provider believes you to be as reliable and honest as a Nigerian eBay bidder. 2. A gateway into a business or market, or a bridgehead, as a more military-minded manager might call it.

Granular/Granularity One of the commonest management-speak words, and yet the English language has no way of actually translating it.

Honcho To approve. Origin, and reason for existing, unknown. Used exclusively by tossers. 'Fancy a pint?' 'I honcho that!'

Hymn Sheet The company's set of goals, from which everyone should be singing. Song sheet is an alternative term, preferred by some as being non-culturally weighted, and therefore not offensive to minorities. It also avoids conjuring up an uninspiring image of boring Sunday mornings spent in the back of church. In both cases it means trying to bring the team together in a dynamic fourth-generation sort of way.

K A thousand. While a city trader might say 'I sacked a faasand norveners today, and made meself faasands,' an executive manager would say 'I facilitated the downsizing of several non-essential parts of the organizational ecosystem, and increased the company's profit margin by several K as a result.'

Key The most important. Possibly the most overused word in MSE.

Killer The really good part of something, such as a killer track on a CD, a killer outfit, or killer quarterly percentiles.

Mission-crucial (or mission-critical)
A computing term referring to a piece of hardware that a company absolutely has to have, lending the IT department the seductive air of an SAS operation behind enemy lines.

Models 1. Ideals, as in an ideal/model society. 2. A less than ideal situation thought up in the boardroom for predicting certain situations, such as the extinction of a species, the world running out of oil by 2020, or even worse, the company going broke in five years. Usually accompanied by a tedious, three-hour long projector slide show and a whole maths book's worth of bar charts, line graphs and Venn diagrams.

Morph 1. In ancient Greece, the legendary ability of a man to take on the shape of a wild beast. 2. In modern Europe and America, the legendary ability of a company to take on the shape of anything it damn well pleases.

Movers and shakers New York-based company tosspots, or those younger and more successful than you.

Niches 1. In the marketplace, a speciality ensuring survival for a poor-quality good, usually by being cheaper or more depraved than its nearest rival, and often therefore a euphemism for the more experimental regions of pornography. 2. In the office, the term used to describe jobs no one wants, and which therefore juniors anxious to ensure their survival will do.

No-brainer A choice so easy even a person with no brain, i.e. someone who works in marketing, can decide on. An American term that sounds as stupid coming from a British person as 'loverly jubbly' might do coming from an Afghan mountain tribesman.

Outcomes An over-used word that can be favourable or unfavourable, referring to either a) possible strands of the far distant future, entwined in the many parallel alternative realities of science fiction, but involving senior account executives rather than superheroes or b) something as mundane as having a good night on the piss. Thus a favourable outcome can apply both to the company's acquisition of a worldwide monopoly on oil, or having a good game of Internet golf.

Positioning Finding a product's place in the market, usually by uncomfortably squashing it between two close rivals. A bit like grumpy travellers elbowing each other for the armrest on the Tube.

Proactive Tautology To take control of a situation by causing something to happen rather than be passive. Originated in 1930s Europe, a time of great proactivity.

R

Results-driven An adjective used to describe a ruthless, horrible, marketing division run by heartless twenty-somethings, destined to die alone, and earning £50,000 a year, £30,000 of which goes on coke.

S

Scale The amount of a finite resource that can be produced from a particular source, before the bloodthirsty-but-co-operative dictator is overthrown by some unhelpful religious nut.

Scalable A product that can be sold or marketed in a number of ways.

Scenario A semi-pornographic fantasy, but with the words 'and one thing led to another, she gently licked his so and so' substituted for 'then quarterly growth jumped 12% without so much as an aggressive advertising push.'

Signage Outdoor branding, such as those Eva Herzivogaza bra ads that used to cause traffic accidents in France, or explicit adverts for dildos that knicker shops seem to think they have the right to force on us.

Systems A popular term with any company, and not really meaning much except 'doing stuff, vaguely'.

Touch base The equivalent of 'mama' for human babies. In other words, the first phrase a company man will learn to use, and a warning siren to others that this individual will be calling in the future, and may to one's horror insist on meeting for lunch occasionally.

Value-added The extra 15% of quality that comes with a product, usually with an extra 20% in price.

TUESDAY

RESOURCES, HUMAN AND OTHERWISE

Once you're sitting in that leather chair with the bend specially designed towards building a managerial posture, you must breathe managerialism 24 hours a day. Before you learn the key words relating to the company you'll now be part of, here is a four-step guide towards the art of leadership.

1. Rebrand yourself. Assuming that no one in your new office will ever have heard of you, convince yourself that you're a real go-getter, tough as nails and an inspired leader. Suppress those memories of having your head flushed down the school toilet.

2. Grovel to everyone above you. Imitate their style of dress, their mannerisms and their taste in music. If they're American, begin to talk with an American twang.

3. Delegate… everything. Except meetings or midweek jollies masquerading as 'forward planning brainstorms'.

4. Say goodbyes to family members; you'll never see them again. You'll be working such extraordinary hours that you'll end up a regular at the hotel closest to work.

BULLSHIT MANAGER'S

TUESDAY SPEAK

Action-items Items needed for a particular action to be implemented i.e. pens, Post-It notes and cups of tea.

Action network As in 'centrally led action network', as certain BBC managers call it. A pen-pusher's powerbase of lackeys, brown-nosers and people with suspiciously similar facial features and surnames.

Applications 1. A piece of software designed to fulfil a purpose on behalf of the company. 2. A piece of human resources designed to fulfil a purpose on behalf of the company.

Architectures A case of managers using a non-existent plural; the structure of something, such as a business, or a hair-brained money-making scheme.

Bottom Line 1. Money. 2. Importance. 3. Both of the above. Taken from the traditional tax sheet, where the bottom line refers to how much your accountant and the government between them have stolen from you. Also, double and triple bottom line, really important, and really, really important respectively.

Broad assets Non-physical assets, such as the goodwill of customers. Also, the nostalgia older people have for your brand, even though they are dimly unaware that it hasn't been made in Britain since 1987, and that the product's avuncular figurehead is in fact a fictional character dreamed up by the marketing department.

Critical inclusion infrastructure
When the National Probation Service was split into 'CLANS' (Centrally Led Action Networks) in 2001, this is what they were said to be part of, though to this day no management-speak expert has managed to translate the term into ordinary English.

Deliverables The fruit of one's work, the end product, the result of all this hard graft, though it doesn't actually have to be an actual physical thing. In the case of a public relations firm, for instance, the 'deliverables' are the 'coverage' a particular product receives in print, cleverly disguised as a piece of journalism by a lazy, drunken hack.

Dependencies A subordinate thing inside a bureaucratic structure. An example would be the one surviving fully-qualified doctor in a hospital, lost among the legions of management guys who, given current rates of growth, will soon outnumber the traditional population of hospitals: clumsy drunks, old malingerers, and accident-prone kids with potties on their heads.

Distributed value chain A chain of events that is supposed to ensure a consistent level of quality from the time the drug-riddled carcasses of thousands of cattle are mashed into one great lump of gristle, to the point

where a harassed young mother buys the
burger and chips for her ADHD-suffering brat.

Functionalities The range of operations
that can be run by a computer or office
worker, as in 'the new Team Manager 4.6,
with functionalities, including added in-built
banter, pre-programmed right-wing views and
a sexual harassment performing upgrade.'

HR Human resources. Company assets
largely made up of carbon, brain matter
and internal organs; humans to be
exploited, used up and then replaced.

Infomediaries 1. The holders of knowledge, similar to ancient Shaman, who alone possessed the secrets of the seasons and the stars. 2. The IT department.

Infrastructures Endless different corporate divisions within an unwieldy government agency, so baffling and labyrinth-like that future civilisations will marvel at their complexity, much in the same way as we gaze at the Pyramids, possibly believing that only aliens could have designed them.

Matrix 1. A sci-fi flick about a nightmarish glass and steel world where nothing turns out to be what it seems. 2. A factual nightmarish glass and steel world where nothing turns out to be what it seems based on an organisational structure where two or more chains of command may lie in one soul-less, Agent Smith-like bureaucrat.

Mesh The huge network of computers in a large company's IT department that strangely resembles the robotic monstrosity from Superman III.

Networks Chains of command and infrastructures, usually accompanied by enough paperwork to stretch from Earth to Mars. What ensures that each worker has a baffling array of different managers to report to.

OB The product. Origins of this term unknown, although the first person to say it was probably called Troy Gentry or Brad Whiteburger, or something similar.

Open source A marketplace where goods are freely available.

Organisational ecosystem Similar to the natural ecosystem, in that the company's large predators eat the medium-sized ones and shit them out, while the digested remains are fought over by even smaller scavengers.

Platforms 1. A term in computing referring to the standard of a piece of hardware, and its compatibility with different types of software. 2. In management, a worker's compatibility with others, i.e. beery, lecherous sexual predator and pregnant feminist.

Purchasers and providers In a large, slow-moving government organisation, the added red tape which is used to departmentalize the company, so that someone can't even borrow a stapler from next door without filling out his divisional cost code on a purchaser-provider form.

Schemas A more technical way of saying model. If your boss ever uses this word, you are in the wrong job.

Silo Individuals who are towers of silence, not sharing information with their colleagues for reasons of economic prudence, or simply because they don't like them. The reality of any multi-national corporation, as illustrated when you ring up the American division of your company, and they don't give a flying toss who you are or where you are, nor could they place you on a map even if they were inclined to do so.

Strategic marketplace For businessmen who like to play RISK in their spare time, the little part of the map where they absolutely have to have a little cannon.

Supply-chain The sequence by which a good is sourced, built, packaged, marketed and sold. Still just a noun at the time of writing, but it's only a matter of time before people are said to be 'supply-chaining'.

Technologies Those magic weapons that are going to come along and save the business, similar to the 'miracle weapon' the Nazis still believed would win the war in April 1945.

Toolbox As in a 'toolbox of components', where ideas go to rest, before never being used, in the wonderful fantasyland of management promises.

Vertical market Where all the potential customers of a particular product are to be found. For example, what lorry drivers are to cigarette paper manufacturers, who make king-sized papers solely for their use, since they need longer roll-ups to keep them going.

Web services The company's Internet set-up, which helpfully blocks anything remotely amusing or arousing from getting sent to staff, such as slide shows of Swedish girls in clubs, drunk Russian miners, or a teenage Star Wars fan doing a dance.

Whiteboard Some sort of computer community where groups of like-minded geeks can exchange ideas, similar to a website message board. Likewise, a forum in which staff get to write down and exchange ideas, which can then be easily removed by a metaphorical teacher's brush.

WEDNESDAY

BRENTISMS

No one's going to take you seriously as a manager unless you can reel off a couple of choice phrases, or know the latest acronyms doing the rounds. Here are a few of the essential terms that should pepper your speech from now on.

BULLSHIT MANAGER'S

WEDNESDAY SPEAK

B

Blue skies thinking A phrase almost mandatory in tax-leeching government departments and quangos. An ability to see the bigger picture, to see the wood from the trees, such as a visionary well worth his £250,000 a year government salary, plus expenses, grace and favour flat in Notting Hill, and generous pension, might have.

Bring to the table One's contribution to a particular enterprise, from Matthew 16:3. 'And the Lord spoke to his favourite John, and asked of him: "So what is Judas bringing to the table?" "My Lord," John spoke, for he was much afeared, "Iscariot has been doing some blue skies thinking recently and is very much outside the box."'

C

CAD 1. What students and governments have in common – a Current Account Deficit. 2. James Hewitt.

Close of play Usually the opening words to a tedious meeting that will stretch over several days, like a painfully long Wagnerian opera. A term borrowed from the money markets, but transferred to the staid world of corporate meetings. Usually used to ask 'so what were you on about yesterday?'

Cooking on gas Going rather well.

D

Ducks in a row Something that can easily be shot at, even by a blind, one-armed Greenpeace campaigner.

E

Ensure results achievement An especially poetic way of saying 'succeeds.'

Exercise in box-ticking A long list of tedious jobs that have to be done.

Going forwards What dynamic, global companies aim for. In fact, the aim of pretty much every body and organism in the entire universe as well.

GOS Gross Operating Share. An early MSE word that has since gone out of use, denoting one's piece of the market pie.

Industrial quality management science The art of evaluating 'quality' from jobs that cannot be measured, such as nursing, teaching or people vaguely involved in the 'caring' industry, using jargon unintelligible to human

kind, and therefore justifying ever-greater
salaries for those involved in the measuring.

J

Jump through hoops To perform a
demeaning and humiliating task for the
benefit of the company director, which
perhaps might eventually be rewarded
with a biscuit and a pat on the head.

Just add water A uniquely smug way of
saying that a product is ready to go, usually
enunciated with a mildly Americanized
accent with all the t's turned to d's.

KBB Key Brand Benefit. What differentiates one particular type of useless gadget from loads of other types of useless gadgets.

KPI Key Performance Indicators – signs of whether you're doing a good job or not. Usually applied to those areas of the public sector where it's impossible to gauge what the department actually does. For example, waiting lists, percentage of teachers maimed by pupils, or number of staff bunking work on any one day in order to go on jollies.

Let's raise it up the flagpole and see if anyone salutes it Let's see if we can get away with this.

Low hanging fruit Something that brings the greatest reward for the least amount of effort.

NIH Not Invented Here; a product that the company refuses to take the blame for.

On the same page 1. In boring meetings, a manager's enquiry as to whether everyone is in agreement with him. 2. In boring meetings, a manager's enquiry as to whether everyone has fallen into a trance back on page 11 of the relevant document.

Oven ready Any product targeted at those twenty-something young professionals too busy to waste their time doing anything after 12 hours of interfacing with a PC.

Push the envelope 1. The action of a boardroom-based romantic hero, the type of maverick who doesn't play by anyone's rules, least of all those of the Monopoly and Mergers Commission. 2. To cross a boundary of the mind, or of taste and morality.

Reconcile the disconnect To fix a problem. A term which originally referred to an accounts problem but adapted by '24-7' managers to refer to anything, e.g. marriage problems, impotence, etc.

Reality check A brief and tentative step outside of the company's parameters to make sure that it is, indeed, the rest of the world that has gone mad, and not those in the boardroom.

ROI An acronym for Return On Investment, which shows the speaker has basic knowledge of MSE and that his three years at Thames Valley Polytechnic weren't wasted.

SME Small/Medium Enterprise. If there were ever going to be a trendy yoof magazine about business, this would be a good title for it.

SOS As in the phrase, 'Let's send out an SOS, put up the red flag and see what comes over the horizon – hopefully the Cavalry.' Or, in the corporate world, 'Call IT.'

Stretch the assignment To work flat-out.

Synthesize the differentials What people do when they get cabbies to exaggerate the fare for the benefit of the receipt.

Take it to the next level Get on with it, for Chrissake.

We're not trying to reinvent the wheel This is something quite easy.

Win-win situation A risky sounding venture that can't go wrong on paper but still leaves you with a nagging, unpleasant doubt in the back of your mind, as it usually involves a hugely generous offer and a bank in Lagos.

THURSDAY

MICRO-MANAGING THE CORE COMPETENCIES: LEADERSHIP

Being a manager is all about being a good leader; someone the staff fear, love, respect, and most importantly, can communicate with. That's assuming that everyone is well versed in MSE; otherwise they won't have a clue what you're on about.

BULLSHIT MANAGER'S

THURSDAY SPEAK

B

Bandwidth Wavelength. As in 'Bearing in mind the architectures we've discussed with the B2B applications in the back-end, is he on the same bandwidth as us?' 'I doubt it, sir, he hasn't got a clue what you're on about.'

Best practice The most successful way of running a business, something top corporate types will pay anything to learn to do, to the extent of paying $1000 to some obvious charlatan who quotes ancient philosophers' take on how to run a company 2,000 years after his death.

Big picture The wider implications, usually explained to a manager suffering an attack of conscience, and usually implying that the ends justify the means, especially if the ends mean the company getting very rich. A term borrowed from Hollywood, the magical place in America where dreams come true.

Big time The height of prestige; for actors, Hollywood; for footballers, the Premiership; for middle-managers, a £75k job high-up some new government body designed to ensure there are the right number of traffic cones in every street.

Brain dump The closing stages of a brainstorm, when all the various flotsam and jetsam floating around the attendees' collective mind is thrown onto a flow chart, in the vague hope that something useful will come of it.

But-in One's thoughts or opinions, as in 'Let's get their but-ins on this one,

Troy.' It implies asking someone's opinion before they inevitably offer it anyway.

Buy-in Exactly the same as 'But-in', which suggests that one arose out of the other simply as a spelling mistake.

C

Champion A figurehead, a sacrificial lamb, and a patsy for any initiative with more than a small risk of going disastrously tits-up.

Channels The various methods by which human beings may talk to each other in the corporate or government world, often with the word 'appropriate' attached. One of many management-speak words with a military history. Or gossip, as it should really be called.

Commit The thing men find most difficult to do, whether to a woman or to a tedious work project.

Collateral A term once used only in relation to things like office premises and expensive machinery, but now applied to envelopes, Post-It notes and paper clips.

Core competencies The bits of your job that the company considers essential, and not the parts you find essential, such as going on eBay, emailing your friends and playing Internet golf. A piece of guff invented for the purposes of the company's personal development review, an annual check up to remind the firm just how many pointless hangers-on it is carrying.

CRM Customer Relations Management. The art of getting some poor mouse-voiced teenager called Kelly from Darlington to answer the complaints line, so that the wronged customer immediately feels like he's shooting Bambi just by complaining about getting gas bills and a court summons from a company he doesn't even use.

Cultivate Often accompanied by 'relationship' and 'reputation'. To take time building up an illusion of goodwill with a client, even though you mutter 'tosser' after putting the phone down every time you speak to them.

Customer deployments sales 4,000 customer deployments per month simply means 4,000 sales per month, but the newer phrase gives the vague impression that the stationery/furniture/PCs or whatever the product in question, are being delivered by a team of US marines.

Customer experience Nowadays customers don't merely pay money for a service, they 'buy an experience.'

Customer-focused Another phrase from the lexicon of corporate Americana, with all the sincerity of a burger bar cashier saying 'Have a nice day' to a smackhead who only came in to shoot up in the toilets.

Division initiatives A plan devised by one part of the company to gain for itself more power and influence. A boardroom struggle straight out of the early days of the Third Reich, but without its efficiency.

Empower/empowerment In public sector jargon, to give the sick and decrepit the choice of which hospital corridor they can lay neglected in for a week before succumbing to an illness they didn't even have when they arrived.

End-to-end Football term normally used to denote an exciting period when goals can be scored by both sides and the fans are pumped up with adrenalin, and therefore a natural phrase to effortlessly slide into the world of middle management. 'Did you listen to that meeting last night? That was really end-to-end stuff.'

Eyeball To stare at a business rival in an unnecessarily macho way with the intention of intimidating, but usually only succeeding

in looking like a pop star looking at an
undercover policeman in a public toilet.

Face time The equivalent of a divorced
father's 'quality time', but with a manager
instead of a father, the end result being
the same awkward, stilted conversation
about where your life is going.

Fora Plural of forum, an ancient and dead
word that has been mysteriously resurrected
in the last decade, for no reason other
than the fact that the word 'places' wasn't
considered mysterious or inaccessible enough.

G

Game plan A strategy worked out in advance by a sales group often thought up in some compulsory and excruciating team bonding session spent in a semi-rustic Holiday Inn.

I

Incubate 1. To sit on a newborn baby like a mother hen, clucking proudly and with a protective glow that only a mother can know. 2. To create a slow-growing business monster that will one day destroy everything around it like some modern-day business-based version of King Kong.

Initiatives With the soul crushing 'government' as a prefix, quick-fire schemes doomed to end in, at best, nothing, and at worst, disaster. Usually used suspiciously soon after a widely publicised cock-up.

Integrate To combine two or more departments into one, usually for the benefit of the people running the new monstrously sized operation. For example, putting John Prescott in charge of a huge government super-ministry running transport, the environment, art galleries and whatever slum is to be renamed as a regeneration zone.

Loop The magic circle, where things are decided, usually a boardroom that could only look more sinister if company policy was reversed to allow smoking.

Magnetic Attractive. Similar in meaning to 'fanny-magnet'. However, this man uses his competent managerial skills (rather than souped-up Cavalier) to have corporate clients, not women, fawning over him (or the product he's selling).

Magnetic North The right direction for a company, the true path that only select visionary-type people can see, as presumably they are armed with some sort of metaphorical compass.

Methodology A term used as a blame-shifting vaccine before announcing the results of some suspiciously convenient 'research' that justifies your latest hare-brained scheme, so that your audience will believe you are a workaholic with an eye for detail, rather than someone hopelessly out of his depth.

Metrics The distance between two objects, though no longer used in its literal mathematical sense, but now referring to a more metaphorical, and therefore more difficult to disprove, distance of the mindset. As a manager might say to a marriage counsellor, 'I feel the metrics between my darling and I have been growing since I had that interface with the lapdancer last year.'

Micro-manage To mollycoddle someone new or clearly not up to the job, like a puppet master.

Mindshare A futuristic sounding version of what used to be called 'knocking your heads together', conjuring up bizarre sci-fi images of a world where telepathy has not just been invented, but is regularly used by marketing departments up and down the land. A brainstorm.

Monetize To express something in the form of a currency, whether relating to a company's web site, social problems or human happiness, for the benefit of those who are totally incapable of understanding anything, even emotions, unless it is explained to them via a children's hand-puppet mime of 'if it were money.'

Networking To restructure an organisation, especially by physically moving desks. Thus the process of clearing out their drawers gives the staff a mildly unpleasant but healthy reminder that you're the only thing that separates them from bankruptcy.

Off line Off the record. Something sensitive that is best not put in an email to all your friends, such as committing unnatural acts with your girlfriend's best friend while watching West Ham on TV.

One-to-one Meeting a client, business partner or government official in the flesh, usually at a very expensive restaurant, when the taxpayers pay for the bill.

Open-plan Describing a system that has few 'walls' to constrain it, and is full of individual creativity and inspiring to work for, just like real-life open plan offices – call centres for example.

Ownability How much of a project can be all yours, or to what extent you have to share the glory, blame and profit with some other idiot.

Partnerships The getting together of two or more firms for an enterprise. In line with the word's growing sexual definition, it often means with the intention of screwing each other, only to feel ashamed and disgusted afterwards.

Relationships The same as in standard English, but without any of the affection, love or empathy that goes with it.

Revisit To go back to a particular step in a project, over and over again. Taken from the psychoanalytic term used for someone deep in trauma.

S

Seize A military sounding word used by executives who've obviously spent too much time reading The Art of War.

Strategic fit An alliance of two businesses that suits both sides, with all the sincerity of the Nazi-Soviet pact.

Syndicate To pay someone else to do one's dirty work – think repayment company that specialises in sending red-inked threatening letters to the hopelessly indebted, with words that should be read out by the actor Ross Kemp.

Visionary A person with imagination, wisdom and leadership abilities; from the Middle English word visionary, meaning not practical, unworkable.

Visualize To make something apparent, even when it is not actually there i.e. the Emperor's New Clothes, France's battle plans, Iraqi nuclear weapons.

FRIDAY

MORNING: VERBING

One of the most vital steps on the road to mastering management-speak is the art of turning everything into a verb. The following words have all been used as verbs in academic papers or management reports, despite all common sense. So don't be restricted. No one will call you a bad manager if you decide to make one up on the spot.

BULLSHIT MANAGER'S

FRIDAY SPEAK

Action In English, a legal term applying to something worthy of legal action; in management-speak, 'to do.' 'Hey Dwight, let's action a few brewskies in the bar, then I honcho a visit to a lap-dancing club for some high level lechery.'

Aggregate To lump a number of people into a particular market, for example ill-educated randy young men in the 18-24 groups, fond of spunking their cash on clothes, holidays and chasing skirt. From the Latin words 'ad', meaning 'to lump together', and 'greg', meaning 'a flock of animals'.

B

Benchmark To compare a rival's efforts against the supposed benchmark, a noun originally taken from the glamorous world of surveying.

D

Dialoguing To talk. Presumably monologuing is what mad people do.

Disintermediate To keep out of a situation. For example, if a management-speaking girl was out on the town with her boyfriend, and he got into a fight, she'd cry out, 'Disintermediate, Gary, he's not worf it.'

Envisioneer To imagine a certain future situation arising, no matter how unlikely, immoral or pointless it may be.

Expedite To take your foot out (this one is best said in the sort of cruel cut-glass English accent found in Mel Gibson films).

Facilitate To make possible, from the French word for 'easy', the sort of verb invented purely for the use of Bond villains and creepy bosses.

Gender In pointless sociology papers, a person who has been bred by society to think that, just because he is a man, he necessarily has to like football, pubs and the workings of car engines.

Grandfather To retire out-of-date products that have no more use to the company. A term obviously invented by men with heavy consciences.

Impact To impact on someone or something. A noun-verb transformation that has long since spread into general English, even making it into Star Wars (as uttered by one of the fat X-Wing fighters destined to die in the battle sequence). In MSE usually used in less heroic situations, such as the task of winning glory in the market place.

Incentivize 1. To encourage staff to work harder by commenting on their children's photos, pointing out how awful it would be for them to start school with an unemployed father. 2. In more progressive institutions around the Square Mile, to give workers generous £1m plus bonuses.

Informationalize To write down.

Input To stick one's tu'pennies' worth into a conversation.

Interface 1. The no man's land between two departments or industries. Once every four years the two sides might meet up to play a game of football, but the rest of the time is spent sniping at each other. 2. A computer terminal. 3. To communicate with another human being in a very inhuman sort of way.

Iterate To say, but using a Latin rather than an English word. Before the Reformation, Catholic priests used Latin to keep the general population ignorant of their doings. The same pretty much applies to our modern-day masters.

J

Journalize To put down on paper.

L

Leverage While the noun applies to the use of a force by a lever, the verb means to use borrowed money to crowbar one's way into the market.

Productize To turn something into a 'product' with its own brand essence and marketability. Often used in reference to a gormless sportsman fond of wearing designer clothes.

Reintermediate To almost go back to basics, but not quite. A polite way of saying 'I stopped listening after about the third sentence.'

Scope To make something bigger.

Strategize To get together to think of a plan of attack. A word so rapidly creeping into mainstream language that soon even bank robbers and anti-paedo mobs will be 'strategizing'.

Synergy/Synergize/Synergistic To group together, to form a relationship, in order that both sides may prosper. A verb uttered only by repulsive 'creative media' people sweating out last night's cocaine binge.

Unitize To turn into one, as in several separate bureaucracies into one super-quango. A modern equivalent of the verb 'to unite', so if middle managers had been responsible for the Declaration of Independence, we'd now have the Unitized States of America.

Utilize To use. Never use a simple English word when a complicated Latin one, using three times as many syllables, will do.

Variablilize To take into account the unpredictable variables when assessing how much of a success or failure your business has been, i.e. claiming that 9/11 has adversely affected your sales, even if you run a fun fair in Swindon.

FRIDAY

AFTERNOON: SOLUTIONS

If you're ever unsure as to what to call the goods or service you are offering, simply add 'solutions' to anything you come up with. The word has become so common that you'll find it in pretty much any situation, as these examples from Private Eye magazine illustrate.

CleanseSmart Gut Solutions
constipation pills

Initial Washroom Solutions
toilets

Addis Cleaning Solutions
mops

NFR Cooling Solutions
fridges

Travel sector solutions company
sick bag manufacturers

Solutions Manager, Yorkshire Water
sewage boss

Motoring and vehicle solutions
breakdown truck

Cyclone Mobility Disabled Solutions
wheelchairs

Storage solutions
plastic boxes

Attachment solutions designed to satisfy
all your attachment requirements
clips

Canape solutions
catering

Klaxon: evacuation solutions
fire alarms

Neat Feet Medical Foot Solutions
chiropody

Doggie solutions
dog leads

Jesus Media Solutions
religious videos

SATURDAY

THE CUTTING EDGE

The greatest insult to any manager is to suggest they're not up to speed with the latest trends. So if you want to earn your £100k a year, learn all the latest Americanisms, psychobabble, and web-based waffle.

BULLSHIT
MANAGER'S

SATURDAY SPEAK

B

Ball Park To be in the same financial region as someone else. One of many baseball terms that has seeped into management-speak, as well as football jargon and the English language in general. Even people who know nothing at all about baseball use it. Other baseball phrases which are now generally used include 'strike one!' (to mean a first attempt), 'leftfield' (to mean strange) and 'second base' (to mean sticking your hand up a woman's bra).

Bimediality A system whereby teams of radio and TV journalists from different departments work under the same bunch of grey, faceless, corporate drones. A word derived from the BBC based management-speak dialectic offshoot, Birtspeak, named after John Birt, the former director-general

and later government-appointed director
of 'blue skies thinking,' known for his
inability to speak anything but jargon.

Bleeding edge A distinct division of a company
that is likely to screw up the remainder of
the business. A word borrowed from the
dashing world of paper font manufacturers.

Clinical governance A piece of jargon from
NHS management, that cumbersome taxpayer-
funded bullshit generator, meaning efficient,
clean and free of waste administration, just like
that found in national health service hospitals.

Closure 1. In America, the sense of relief one
gets when a murderer is executed. In England

the sense of relief one gets when a murderer gets six years with the possibility of being out in three. 2. The sense of relief a manager feels when a deal is finally closed... and there won't be any more awkward questions.

Cross-media A term used in the tosspot circles of advertising types, meaning to run a campaign on billboards and in magazines at the same time as on TV and radio slots. Often used with some ultra-trendy viral Mpeg thrown in just for fun.

Cross-platform 1. A piece of software that can be used on different types of computers. 2. Likewise, an office drone that can be used in any situation. A business version of the Dutch philosophy of total football, but without Johann Cruyff.

CSR Corporate Social Responsibility. Usually expressed by giving a couple of grand at the end of the tax year to some charity, carefully chosen for its appeal to the key female 30-something demographic. Puppies with big eyes, Spanish donkeys, that sort of thing.

Customized Adapted. As, for example, in made to suit the gaudy tastes of 13-year-old ratboys a firm is targeting. This could take the form of adding 100 tinny, annoying ring tones to a mobile phone, with some mildly titillating image of a low-rent topless model thrown in.

Cutting-edge Of a technology. To be modern and up to date, but with the sinister implication of having some prize twat of a Hoxton artist on-board somewhere, probably to design a mobile phone cover specially made for men over 30 who really should grow up.

Diversity To stick a couple of ethnic minorities on the brochure, and throw in a gay person or two while you're at it.

e-enable To turn on one's computer, or to call the IT department.

e-business Porn.

e-commerce Emails sent by mystery Africans asking for a loan of $26m, which they promise to pay back once the rebels have been repelled from their property.

e-markets Compulsive masturbators chained to their left-hand mouse, wiping their shame away in squalid, tissue-padded bedrooms. Put another way, the aspirational, 18-30, male, non-cohabiting, one-income/no-dependents sector.

Embrace To make money out of some demographic disaster, as in 'This cutting edge media centre will **Embrace** the growing number of the young male demographic too thick to read.'

Emotional intelligence Outside the office, an area of IQ that women claim as their own, as a counter to the traditional male strong points of doing puzzles, reading manuals and understanding football league tables. In MSE, the ability to take a bollocking without crying.

Engage To develop a piece of technology even more obtrusive or annoying than its exceptionally annoying predecessor. For example, a picture phone that makes pulling a sickie impossible.

Enhance/enhancement To make something better, but in a cutting-edge, modern sort of way. The extra component that a sales assistant is trained to flog to the customers, by pointing out that their original piece of equipment is fairly useless unless they fork out for this extra bit.

Exploit Used increasingly in the sense of to exploit a growing trend (see embrace), rather than in the sense of not taking advantage of poor and hungry Third World types.

Extensible A mixture of 'extendable' and 'sensible'. Probably.

Fiduciary Financial responsibility, that's
to the shareholders, not the staff.

Frictionless A government policy that
doesn't result in lorry drivers blocking roads,
or in rioting taking place in the streets,
or in John Prescott punching anyone.

Generate To whip-up an interest in
something that people had no use for until
now. For example, a manufactured pop
group made of up four brainless yahoos, each
with a distinctive personality that has been
allocated to them by the record company.

Global Term usually followed by words such as 'markets', 'strategy' or 'domination.'

Grow 1. What successful businesses do. 2. What tiresome public sector bureaucracy bosses encourage their employees to do, in an emotional and spiritual sense.

Harness A form of modern alchemy, where demographic trends are turned into pure gold. For example, a marketing firm can harness the nation's growing number of depression sufferers into a market for drugs, artificial sunlight lamps and junk food.

Holistic 1. An approach to medicine that looks at all things as being inter-connected, and

attempts to treat aspects of the spirit rather than the actual illness, with dubious results.
2. An approach to business that looks at all things as being inter-connected, attempting to treat aspects of the spirit rather than facing up to the actual problem, with dubious results.

Innovate To fiddle around with, a useful buzzword to use around any workplace obsessed with change. Not to innovate implies being a dinosaur, and we all know that they failed to survive.

Interactive Something that allows some two-way participation, especially when it involves text messages at £1.20 per throw. Popular in porn, the only area of life where

men are desperate enough and drunk
enough to spend a horrifying amount to see
a couple of foul-mouthed single mothers
slap each other's arses on late night TV.

Issues In America, the feelings of a
spoilt, self-obsessed, twenty-something,
show biz type. In the corporate world,
the feelings of a company's division.

Knowledge-based Adjective applied to an
economy reliant solely on IT, financial services
and up-market chain pubs, e.g. Britain. Other
similar terms are **knowledge manager**,
knowledge mobilization, and **knowledge
localization**, all of which mean precisely sod all.

Leading edge In aeronautics, a wing or propeller blade; in management-speak, the forefront of technological development, and what every media tit will be carrying in 2007.

Next generation The irritating, all-looks-and-no-substance new crop of gadgets aimed at the irritating, all-looks-and-no-substance new crop of worthless boy-band hopefuls who make up the younger generation of most Western democracies.

No blame culture An inclusive and supportive workplace where employees aren't encouraged to immediately 'cover their ass' every time something goes wrong. The very opposite to the traditional Japanese martial tradition, where the second in command cuts out his own innards out if quarterly sales drop by so much as 3%.

Orchestrate To cause something to happen. Whereas in standard English this term has a pejorative meaning, implying the machinations of a shadowy cabal, in management-speak it's seen as a positively good thing.

Plug-and-play Another term borrowed from the rich lexicon of computers, meaning to stick a lead between a digital camera and a computer, so that pictures can be automatically transferred. How a business can be plug-and-play is, frankly, anyone's guess.

Portals Magical rooms that allow you to jump three levels in computer games. Sadly non-existent in real life, but a popular word to use when describing all sorts of web-based customer interactions.

Plurality A local government initiative that brings on board a range of different groups within the community, like radical feminists and Islamic fundamentalists, with hilarious results.

Real-time The ability of computers to process billions of different pieces of information instantly, and to make sense of them, without complaining about working hours.

Revolutionize To change an area of the economy, usually by finding a way of doing the same job with a lot fewer people. Like a social revolution, but where the bosses overthrow the workers.

Self-actualisation To realise your true potential, by becoming a Senior Marketing Manager and finally putting behind you bitter childhood memories of unpopularity, bullying and pant-wetting.

Sexy In business, a word used only in reference to a mobile phone, a digital camera or an MP3 player, and never to an actual human being.

Show-stopper The centrepiece of a new company's product launch. Usually a gadget so bloody cutting-edge that no one but the top 10% of the most gadget-savvy, Japanese school kids, aged 10-12, can understand how to work it. Presented to the world's media from HQ in Los Angeles by the firm's sinister geek boss, with an ultra cool soundtrack of the latest Coldplay track in the background, or whatever band is big at the time.

So-what The important bit, the essence of something. As in 'What's the "so what?"

to that?", best said with an American-style head movement and a 'loser' sign.

Transform To change a business or marketplace, a handy word to use in any meeting or mission statement for a company. The opposite of stagnate.

Unleash To unveil a product, however mundane, with the implication that it is akin to a gun or a penis, and is rock hard.

User-centric Any technology-based product that won't have the owner screaming in frustration, ripping out his hair and smashing his fist down on the offending item, shouting 'Do as I say, you bastard!'

Viral Video streaming ads designed specifically for Internet use. In this way, rather than having to shell out on a TV slot, a company relies on bored office workers to forward its message on to their friends, unaware that they are doing the company's bidding.

Virtual As in 'reality', the fantasy world where its creator can live out his dream, whether that be fighting in World War Two, living in the Playboy mansion, or becoming a CEO of a NASDAQ-rated corporation.

Web-enabled CIA-style technology, whereby a mobile phone can log onto the Internet, so that even if you're up in the Andes, your boss can still find you.

Web-readiness A term left over from the late 1990s dot.com boom, when it was believed the Internet was going to make everyone a fortune. At that time, even a website chronicling the corner flags of the North-east Counties League might go for £3m. Nowadays, it is assumed that since almost every nutter has his own website, even the smallest company will have one.

Wireless World-class Like an old fashioned radio, but presumably a lot better.

SUNDAY

OUTSOURCED, OFFSHORED, SACKED

Finally, there may come a time when things aren't going too well, and you'll have to take aside a trusted employee and frankly admit to him that his job has been outsourced. Your final lesson in bullshit is the most important: this is a tough world, and you'll need to sugar your language from time to time.

BULLSHIT MANAGER'S

SUNDAY SPEAK

Capability gap The difference between what someone thinks of their own abilities, and what everyone else thinks of them.

Deathcare industry The modern term for the business of morticians, undertakers, funeral directors and drunken gravediggers.

Disconnect A verb meaning that something does not add up. Frequently used when referring to a company's tax figures.

Disinternalize To hire someone from outside the company, at huge expense, to

come and make changes that will result
in the inevitable loss of 'internal' jobs. Six
months later the management will re-hire
the people it has fired, to do the same job as
they were doing before, but on temporary
contracts and without a pension scheme.

Downsize To sack half the workforce.

Dynamic Young, inexperienced and ruthless.
Term used to refer to a marketing team fresh
out of the education system. Someone who
is prepared to dress their grandmother up
as a lapdancer and leave her outside Tesco
all day in order to sell 'the product.'

Dynamic learning curves/cultures A school,
department or government operation that on
paper is improving at a rapid rate, but only
because it was absolutely dreadful to start with.

Dynamic market forces The conditions of the global economy, which you are blaming for your failure to perform, rather like a sportsman blames the weather for his poor performance.

E

Efficient A term used to refer to a company that runs with low variable costs, especially those that could be reductionized by a few P45 slips.

Emerging markets India, China and other parts of the Third World where the locals have acquired new wealth but as yet aren't aware of all the junk they can spend it on.

Enterprise Tax-avoidance, out-sourcing or doing a Phil Mitchell-style insurance

job on your company premises. Also,
Enterprise Resource Management – the
ability to get by on less money.

Entry level Crap, rubbish and cheap. In
mobile phone terminology, a term used to
describe a phone that is going to earn a child
the contempt of his classmates, including the
school muggers, because it can't store 10,000
songs or monitor Iran's nuclear programme.

Evaluating The human resources equivalent
of walking around the office, casually
carrying an axe while pointing at people,
muttering 'eenie meenie miny moe.' In other
words, deciding who gets the boot next.

Evolving A verb used to refer to an
employment system based on Charles
Darwin's theory on the survival of the

species, and some of his more radical German followers of the 20th century.

Evolving globalization A term used to describe the firing of an entire peasant class of desk jockeys, in the style of a Soviet cull, and the giving of their jobs to workers in Sri Lanka on one-tenth of their salary.

Executive champion The champion of all sacrificial lambs, chosen from the higher echelons of the company to take the blame for something called Project Titanic or similar disasters.

Flexible An adjective used to denote a service that can be moved from London to Delhi quicker than the Tardis.

Growth moment A desperate straw-clutching exercise in futility used by the CEOs of companies that are going to the wall.

Guests People who used to be called either workers or customers. On cross-Irish Sea ferries for example, 'guests' are asked to stand outside on a freezing, sea-drenched deck if they wish to smoke.

Impactful An adjective used to describe something that will have massive repercussions in the future, such as global warming, high interest rates, or the misuse of English grammar.

Implement To actually carry out the dirty work and impossibly stupid ideas thought out by blue skies thinkers. A neutral, bland, sort of word, popular with a generation of New Labour politicians who have grown up speaking nothing but management-speak English.

Mission statement An official declaration of a company's values, with all references to profits, Sri Lankan sweat shops and Cayman Islands tax declaration, discreetly left out.

Nearshoring A verb very similar to offshoring, except for subtle geographic differences. If your job goes to India, it's offshoring; if it goes to East Kilbride, it's nearshoring.

Outsized Something that has grown extremely large, as in the chief executive's stiffy when he hears about the latest annual profits.

Outsource To bring in some expert management consultants to tell you to implement huge redundancies, in order to make savings that barely cover their fees.

Paradigm shift A huge, momentous change undertaken by a company, often heading to a destination unknown, but which will certainly involve thousands of lackeys getting the boot.

Pinch point The moment when a company starts to notice that things aren't going too well. For example the instant the chairman drowns while on a yachting holiday, having spunked the entire pension fund first.

Processology territory A chaotic period between the rules of two bureaucratic tyrants in a government bureaucracy. A Labour party word.

Recontextualize To understand something in terms of its surroundings. A politician's response to news that a particular police force or hospital has spent more on diversity managers and conference weekends than it has on doing its job.

Redefine A verb used by the media to mean making a market even more lowbrow than it already was by appealing to the lowest common denominator, thereby forcing one's rivals to ditch anything with a smattering of intelligence. For example, a news bulletin announcing: 'Celebrity Arse Shaving has redefined the reality TV market since its launch last autumn. Since then, it's been joined by a host of imitators including Slagfest Island and Celebrity Concentration Camp.'

Reinvent To take an unpalatable product or person and give them a glossy sheen. For example, to present the unfortunate incident where someone kicked his girlfriend in the head in such a way as to make it recede in the distance.

Repurpose A euphemism meaning something a firm does to gloss over a disastrous period in which its name has become synonymous with bad customer service, shoddy business practices, and everything that is wrong with Britain today.

Right-sized A phrase coined in 1988 by the vice-president of General Motors personnel department, Roy S. Roberts, who decided that the euphemism 'downsizing' itself needed a euphemism.

Robust Someone willing to put up with bullying, poor pay and sexual harassment in return for being allowed to crawl one more step up the corporate ladder.

S

Scope creep An out of control project, one that starts off as a part-time job for one lowly assistant, and ends up sucking up 10% of the whole nation's GDP.

Seamless An adjective used to describe how a bureaucratic monolith could blend into another. The way the Health Service and Social Services merge into one seamless 'Society' jobs page in The Guardian.

Slippage Uselessness on an industrial scale, often costing millions or billions of pounds to correct.

Sticky An adjective describing prices or wages that can be increased or decreased without too much impact on demand. Also known as elasticity. For example, football match tickets going up in price by about 1000% over the last 15 years, and demand still increasing, suggests that a) football is very sticky and b) the fans are idiots.

Take ownership To take the blame.

Target To aim at something. What a company or government body hopes to achieve by 2014, or at least at some point in the future when the pensions of all concerned have been secured.

Termination A term for sacking that sounds almost like a reverse euphemism, reminiscent of the sort of downsizing methods used by Bond villains involving shark tanks. Employees learn of their fate through **termination interviews**.

Transition A period of failure following a period of success. Often a transition from a going business to a bankrupt business.

Transparent Something which is open to public scrutiny. For example, a government announcement following a terrible scandal involving a minister, who is punished by being sent off to Brussels to wield more power on twice the salary he had before.

Workshopping A verb describing the process whereby instead of taking a call centre to India, an Indian techie is brought to the West and paid wages that would make him a man about town in Bangalore. Also known as **bodyshopping**.

SUGGESTED READING

If you want to learn more about the art
of management, don't stop here. Listed
now are just some of the books available
in the USA for boardroom ball-breakers
wanting to learn from the masters.

The Leadership Secrets of Attila the Hun
Wess Roberts

How Would Confucius Ask For a Raise? 100
Enlightened Solutions for Tough Business Problems
Carol Orsborn

A Higher Standard of Leadership:
Lessons from the Life of Gandhi
Keshavan Nair

Make It So: Management Lessons from
'Star Trek the Next Generation'
Bill Ross

*The Executive Mystic: Psychic
Power Tools For Success*
Barrie Dolnick

*The Tao of Leadership: Lao Tzu
Tao te Ching for a New Age*
John Heider

*Shakespeare in Charge: The Bard's Guide to
Leading & Succeeding on the Business Stage*
Norman Augustine & Kenneth Adelman

*Corps Business: The 30 Management
Principles of the U.S. Marines*
by David H. Freedman

*Leadership Sopranos Style: How to
Become a More Effective Boss*
by Deborrah Himsel

NOTES ON THE AUTHOR

Ed West has spent most of his adult life in offices, often staring blankly out at the blue skies, thinking about absolutely nothing, while some marketing man explained the key brand benefits he had to offer.

He'd like to thank Emma Grove for all her help, and suggests that if you want to find out more about the world of bullshit, you read Francis Wheen's *How Mumbo-Jumbo Conquered the World,* and *Don Watson's Gobbledygook.*

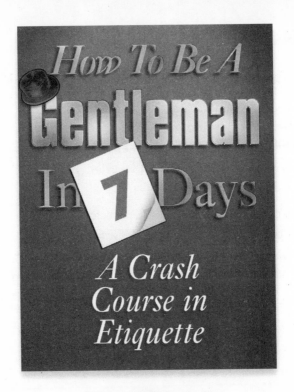

How To Be A
Gentleman
In **7** Days

*A Crash
Course in
Etiquette*

ISBN 1-905102-16-X
£4.99

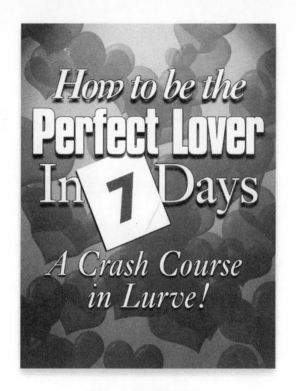

How to be the
Perfect Lover
In 7 Days

A Crash Course
in Lurve!

ISBN 1-905102-77-1
£4.99

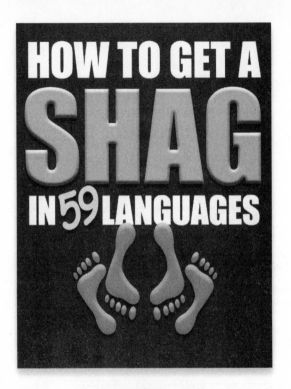

ISBN 1-905102-40-2
£4.99

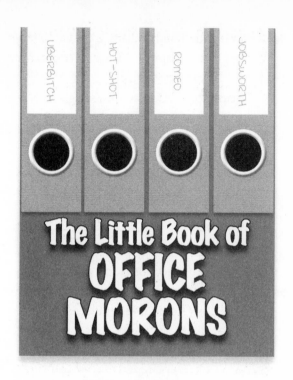

The Little Book of
OFFICE
MORONS

ISBN 1-905102-28-3
£2.99